Advance Praise

"This is a collection that is wandering the halls in the night with a candle threatening to go out. Wytovich taps into the brutal and magical experience of motherhood with poems that are lush and barbed, connecting the maternal with the feral in ways that are unexpected and unforgettable."
—Patricia Grisafi, PhD, author of *Breaking Down Plath* and *Animal*

"What witchcraft is this? These poems are somehow delicate as lace yet razor sharp. Lovely yet venomous. Visceral and emotional, eerie and honest. This collection is essential and in perfect conversation with Shirley Jackson's Blackwood Sisters."
—Rachel Harrison, national bestselling author of *Cackle* and *Black Sheep*

"…an uncomfortable collection. Petal-pressed and pulsing with politeness, her poetry is unflinching in its honesty, each poem a bewitchingly beautiful slurp at the horror of motherhood. A devastating work."
—Lee Murray, five-time Bram Stoker Award winner, co-author of *Tortured Willows*

"…a birth announcement, a lullaby, a eulogy. It is the beautiful, yet painful tangled parts of transformation. Wytovich conjures a sympathetic magic spell, and stands firm as one of the masters of speculative poetry."
—Cynthia Pelayo, Bram Stoker Award-winning author of *Crime Scene*

"…as decadent and surprising as blackberries themselves: often succulent and sometimes tart, always potent enough to leave a stain. Stephanie Wytovich is synonymous with dark poetry."
—Lindy Ryan, Bram Stoker Award-nominated editor of *Into the Forest* and author of *Bless Your Heart*

"With sugar, shadow, and verses sharp as thorns, *On the Subject of Blackberries* will become a sacred text to everyone whose teen witch phase grew into an unapologetic lifestyle…Wytovich channels Merricat with all her complex shapes & secrets, creating a collection that haunts you long after you set it down. Every poem left me breathless, and more deeply bewitched."—Jessica McHugh, two-time Bram Stoker Award® Nominated author, *The Quiet Ways I Destroy You*

"Wytovich finds beauty in the wound as much as in the freshly healed scar, and it is that acceptance of the darkness which adjusts our focus and changes our perspective on emotional and physical trauma. Her brutal honesty makes this work engaging, provocative, and healing. That is some profound magic to put on the page."
—Scott Bradley, Podcaster, Owner *Hellbent for Horror*

"Dark, lovely, and brutal, these poems are a tribute to Shirley Jackson and a hymn for the inner Blackwood sister who resides in all of us. Fans of gothic horror will devour Wytovich's stunning collection in one sitting."
—Jessica Drake-Thomas, author of *Burials* and *Bad Omens*

"Wytovich discloses the festering secrets of her darkest thoughts with the inevitable doom of Emily Dickinson and the dread-infused paranoia of Poe's 'Tell-Tale Heart.' Recommended for lovers of the exquisitely macabre."
—Lee Allen Howard, author of *The Covenant Sacrifice*

"Brilliant and beautiful, *On the Subject of Blackberries* is a worthy companion to Shirley Jackson's classic, *We Have Always Lived in the Castle*. Everything I'd hoped it would be and more."
—Gwendolyn Kiste, Lambda Literary and Bram Stoker Award-winning author of *Reluctant Immortals* and *The Rust Maidens*

"A haunting collection that blends urgency alongside the myth of pastoral, the supernatural, and the body. Stephanie Wytovich's collection is a cacophony of seeking out darkness in light and light in darkness. Each line comes together in a dazzling cemetery of selves—past and present—seeking a rebirth into something truly extraordinary. If Wytovich's words are a match, then this book is the flame."
—Stephanie Valente, author of *Internet Girlfriend*

On the Subject of Blackberries

On the Subject of Blackberries © 2023 by Stephanie M. Wytovich

Published by Raw Dog Screaming Press
Bowie, MD
All rights reserved.
First Edition

Cover art & book design: Jennifer Barnes

Printed in the United States of America
ISBN: 9781947879-84-3

Library of Congress Control Number:
2023943571

RawDogScreaming.com

Also by Stephanie M. Wytovich

Fiction
The Eighth

Poetry
Hysteria
Mourning Jewelry
An Exorcism of Angels
Brothel
Sheet Music for My Acoustic Nightmare
The Apocalyptic Mannequin

Non-Fiction
Writing Poetry in the Dark (editor)

On the Subject of Blackberries

Stephanie M. Wytovich

For Evelyn June

I love you.

I love you.

I love you.

Author's Note

I was a ghost existing in the corner of my house. I had been locked away writing poems while covered in vomit, the scent of sour milk strong on my skin. There was usually dirt under my fingernails, my mascara was always smeared, and I often changed my shirt four times a day, the smell of exhaustion forever ripe on my breath. There were days when writing seemed impossible, and yet other days, it fell out of me, desperate, hungry, begging. This collection became a portrait of postpartum writing, a mirror held up against a new mother struggling with PPD, newly diagnosed with OCD, and someone attempting to love themselves the same way they loved, and continue to love (maybe even more), their perfect cherub of a daughter: Evelyn.

Those first few months were endless nights. I felt like I was disappearing into the couch, my body broken, bruised, unable to fold, stand, or cry. I was afraid to close my eyes, my anxiety so bad that I rarely let go of Evie. It wasn't long after we brought her home that rain poured from our ceilings, our home collapsing in an on-spot metaphor for how I felt inside. We weren't able to use her nursery (or the second floor of our house) and were instead banished to the first floor where I lived next to her bassinet for three months, never leaving the house, not even for a piece of sun.

Next to me through it all was the book We Have Always Lived in the Castle by Shirley Jackson. My favorite novel, my comfort read, my beacon in the dark. I read passages of it to Evie when she had trouble falling asleep. I listened to it on audiobook when I could steal away for a shower now and again. When I made myself tea, I hummed nursery rhymes about blackberries and poison, and while I recognize this sounds scary, that's probably because it was.

You see, I have felt alone for most of my life, but nothing could have prepared me for the loneliness I felt during, and immediately after, my pregnancy. Yes, there were people who were wonderful and who went above and beyond to make me feel loved, but I often felt like Constance and Merricat sitting in the kitchen of their burned house, their doors and windows boarded up while they cowered on the ground afraid of the outside world and everyone in it.

If you know anything about the Blackwood Sisters, if you know anything about me, you know that my obsession has always been with Merricat, that feral wonder of a girl who embraced the thin spaces of our world and watched them bleed into the next, her magic a special type of power that came from rage, from repression, from all those moments she was told to behave, to be quiet, all those nights she was sent to bed without supper. She's always spoken to me, a girl who never felt like people took her seriously, who even after giving birth, still felt treated like a child.

Yes, on the subject of blackberries, I am quite familiar. I became a wolf this past January, the snow a blanket that covered me as I gave birth in a room filled with the screams and howls of labor. I grew fangs and claws as I was cut open, my womb a portal, a land filled with blood magic and moons. I didn't realize that a part of me died then, but she did, maiden to mother, my little girl the most important, beautiful thing. My old self had gone and, in her place, stood this untamable, wild thing with eyes only for her young, and it scared me at first, but then brought me this immense, cleansing peace.

I've been angry for a long time about a lot of different things but when they handed me her little body, I felt more able to challenge, understand, and most importantly let go of everything I've held on to for 30+ years for no other reason than I didn't want it to spill out and ever hurt her. Through pain came relief, a stitched blessing that left scars as a boundary, as a reminder of the person I no longer was or cared to be.

There's witchcraft in that confrontation: a binding spell, a sigil of protection. Evie gave me the strength to water and nourish the garden in my chest, to put flowers in my hair, and to laugh because it just feels good to be alive. In a lot of ways, finishing this book feels like taking a breath of fresh air, embarking on a new beginning.

It's just that this time, I won't have to take that journey alone because there's forever a little hand holding on to mine.

The two of us, against the world.

Blackberries and sugar.

With only the memory of poison.

—Stephanie M. Wytovich, June 3, 2022

The Witchcraft of Writing

By Stephanie M. Wytovich

Like most writers, I carry a notebook. You'll often find me scribbling words or phrases in between elevator rides, or furiously texting a stream of nefarious thoughts into my phone during a conversation, and that's usually where most of my poetry ideas begin. I cobble ideas together, Frankenstein nightmares, and in the end, I have a moment, a picture, an emotion…something I can work with.

That's not what happened here.

My last collection, *The Apocalyptic Mannequin*, came out in 2019, a few months before the pandemic hit. Since then, poetry has been a quiet muse. Sure, I found myself drawn to her on occasion, but my head was otherwise occupied, the séance of our relationship long-since fizzled out. But then I gave birth, a wild experience of scalpels and discarded body parts, clotted blood and newborn cries. When I woke up from surgery, the world looked different, *was* different. I was stitched together, bound to the bed, and when I closed my eyes, I heard nothing but screaming.

I stopped seeing myself in the mirror after that, heard voices in the attic at night. In a lot of ways, I was existing between the veil, transitioning from maiden to mother, my body an empty house, a savage garden. I would look at my daughter and cry over her beauty, her absolute perfection, but when I left her side, the ghosts started to whisper…

…and they said *horrible* things.

This was an emotionally confusing time for me. I would spend my days singing Disney songs to my daughter while she watched sensory videos or listened to ASMR. I read her fantastical stories, took naps near her bassinet, and lovingly fed her while our eyes locked on each other's, and we smiled at our growing bond. Life with her was perfect, but when the sun went down, or when my husband or a grandparent took her in their arms, I felt myself start to itch. My skin crawled with paranoia. I paced in my office, picking at my skin. I worried the pandemic would get into our house, that without me, she wasn't safe.

In another life, I would have prayed, and I suppose in some ways I did. I lit black candles, sought comfort in my cards. I slept with amethyst under my pillow, put selenite above my doors. I stopped sleeping, overwhelmed with depression, anxiety, and intense weeping spells that wracked my body and brought me to the floor. I drank coffee at 3 a.m., counted my baby's breaths, binge-watched true crime documentaries and never left the house. Somewhere around the one-month mark, I knew I needed someone to talk to, someone whose voice was familiar, who knew what it felt like to exist in the thin spaces …

….isolated, feral, and bleeding.

That's when I turned to *We Have Always Lived in the Castle* by Shirley Jackson.

Now this was not my first encounter with the Blackwood sisters. In fact, we had met many, many times before. That's part of the reason I chose them. We had a kinship, a mutual understanding with each other. I kept their secrets, and they kept mine, and as long as we existed in the garden together, Merricat promised not to poison me.

Their story was familiar, comforting even. That might feel like a weird choice of words for those who have read the book, but I found, and continue to find, their sisterhood and their underlying wickedness quite soothing. There's a quiet violence there. A polite horror. The tone matched the emotions swirling in my gut, the ones that reminded me of the blackberries in my fridge, the letter opener in my office.

The more I read the book, the more I found myself scribbling notes in the margins, underlining words, circling small repetitions. I highlighted my favorite passages, continued chapters in automatic writing exercises I held during the night, and one morning when the sun came up, I asked myself: *what do I need to protect myself and my family?*

The answer, as it so often is, was poetry.

I've made no secret in my career about how poetry has been a large part of my mental health self-care routine. Before I could even think about writing, I knew I needed to sit down with my husband and have a long, uncomfortable, serious talk about what I was experiencing and what I felt I needed to do to start fighting my way out of the woods again. The next step I took after talking to him was securing a therapist who I could meet with weekly to help me process my emotions, unpack residual birth trauma, and hopefully start my healing journey. What I wasn't expecting, however, was to be put back on medication, be diagnosed with a panic disorder and OCD, and be recommended for intensive outpatient therapy. Joke was on me though because I couldn't get a single doctor, psychiatrist, or outpatient facility in the area to even return my phone call, let alone discuss admitting me, so my choices, once again, were limited to me and my therapist, and me and the page.

I worked out a writing routine I was comfortable with, something that gave me some alone time but also didn't exacerbate my fear of being away from my daughter, a fear that existed even when we were in the same place. This was a hard but necessary and healthy step in creating distance and breaking panic cycles, and it also helped me reshape my identity again. Those moments in my office were transcendental. I lit incense, hovered over my oracle deck, listened to dark classical music, and dove deep inside Jackson's book. I even got a blackberry wreath tattooed on my shoulder when everything was said and done, but I realize I'm getting ahead of myself.

We haven't even discussed the murder yet.

See, Merricat is my favorite character in literature, and I've given a lot of thought to why that is. She's unapologetic, she's childish, she's stubborn, and somewhat unlikeable. She's also a witch, an outcast, and her actions have earned her the status and start of becoming an urban legend in town. What a woman, am I right? This is what I love to see in literature. I want to see strength and fire and this brutal need to live without worry or care, but what makes Merricat particularly interesting is that despite all the above, she's also *deeply* afraid. Now this isn't a character study and the poems in this collection aren't in Merricat's voice. They aren't even, arguably, in her or Jackson's universe. They are poems inspired by, in response to, and divined from postpartum depression. I just used Jackson's book to help start the conversation.

Let me explain.

I didn't sit down with an intention to write this book and once it started happening, I didn't intend to publish it. These were poems and lines and moments that were raw and vulnerable and scary, and they were born out of exhaustion, rage, and intense grief. I looked at myself as a woman haunting her house, and I sought solace in the Blackwood mansion. I mentioned previously that I treated the book like a puzzle. I took those repeated words and sprinkled them throughout poems as a type of conjuring. I closed my eyes and flipped through the book and let my finger land on a word. I would read that sentence, that page, and I would write to it, alongside it. I spent time in my head creating poison gardens and brick towers, and at night, I'd go outside and look at the moon. I wrote constellations into poems, spilled nightmares onto pages, and found poetry within chapters and symbolism, underneath the dead family members whose corpses we never got to meet.

I would lay in my office, turn the lights off, and light frankincense and myrrh. I would listen to the audiobook with my eyes closed and start to meditate with headphones that pumped brown noise into my head. For months, I was always *near* the castle, but I was also building my own. I would wake from these sessions and automatically write for sprints of five to ten minutes. My hands hurt so bad after doing it—and after doing it repeatedly for so long—I eventually needed to put a numbing cream on my hands and wrists and wear a brace. I bought a notebook and started to collage, cutting up pictures and blacking out words, making poetry out of headless bodies and soft spring flowers. When that failed, I went to my cards. I used a variety of tarot and oracle decks, and I got in the habit of picking one and writing to it. It was my own way of bringing shadow work into my poetry, and it helped prevent me from wanting to hide.

Postpartum is humbling. I burned bay leaves with intentions written on them, did floor washes, and deep cleaned my house with peppermint. I tried everything to find myself in the depression, to wake up from the graveyard in my head, and I learned that motherhood is a strange, terrifying place and it's as beautiful as it is ugly. I wrote some of these poems with my daughter screaming in the background, and others one-handed while she slept angelically in my arms. No matter how bad or dark things got in my head, the shining light behind all of it was my little girl's laugh, her smile, her tiny hand in mine.

She was, and remains, my miracle.

See, mothers are not one thing, and it's foolish to pretend to be. I can, and have been, monstrous and magical and beautiful and kind, and none of that makes me less-than or unworthy of love. I've always lived in the grey, in the in-between, and I'm comfortable there. It keeps me guessing, growing, and learning, and when I need a little help putting my thoughts into words, I know that poetry is waiting for me.

Well, poetry and a little magic.

A funeral of pregnant moons.

1

My name is
werewolf, death-cup,
noise.

I say "Good morning"
to flowers underneath
library books,
drink black coffee to
the foundation of pictures
left on the shelves,

a place built up with layers
against the world   the sky wishing
opposite the village—

    Empty, deserted:

their children an invitation
to my hate.

I have always screamed,
screamed   a long still minute
a flock of taloned hawks
striking, gnashing
at the grocery's door

You watch, transfixed,
perfectly straight, stiff
a carton of spilled milk,
a spoiled rack of lamb:

> my hands, a shopping list
> for locked doors, rotting hearts,
> heaps of golden coins

Yet

through the door
there was a little laugh,
a minute wrapped, waiting,
ready to deliver me home,

> their hateful words a cracked
> cup, a bloodied yolk, the last
> bag of sugar.

How I wished them all dead.

My goal was a deep breath
my thoughts unbearable

> *so much noise*
> *unending noise*

The demons found a way in
opened their eyes in broken plates

> glanced at me,
> smiling.

Those poor girls in the garden
had always been there—
haunted, ghastly,
openly disliked:

    two shadows against
    black woods and gossip.

They stood strong on broken
feet, voices cracked, the hum
of fruit flies stuck in their throats

    just watching, waiting
    six feet deep

I built the fire in the yard
instead of in my bed, but this

desire

to drink gas, to swallow
the match still smoking:
    how beautiful it would be

to die.

I wondered if a cup of tea
could make them stop

if changing the poison
would burn them faster:

    a thousand flames
    inside a flower, an herb.

The boneyard waiting,
begging them to sleep.

II

She stood inside the four corners
securely in sunlight—

                         smiling,

a fairy princess against
my unwelcoming face
precious, with quiet respect.

I gathered mushrooms, ripped
worms from apples, my skin
a study of cigars,
a Sunday-morning sermon,
    biblical, frightening

The cat whispers, tracks mud
from the creek, you call on me
a daughter, an orphan—
           a song spoke quietly
           between tears.

They offered us
a cutting from a rose bush,
a winged horse,

played the harp against
mirrors and sparkling glass.

For six years, I believed
in summer windows,
blue silk drapes, diamonds

at the end of mother's favorite
broom. Your wedding cake

a portrait of nightmares,
this lovely room, untidy
quiet,

the taste of rum and silver
precisely on time.

I slipped into the forest
a complex ballet,
    graceful, unapologetic
each stride   a touch eccentric

your name
a secret, an unexpected question
    withdrawn, chilled
the taste of your penance
a deviation

I force my body into a kindness
curse into the blinds

It was still winter
she was listening and smiling,
almost surprised I could not breathe

    g a s p g a s p g a s p

I broke, left behind
pieces of small tremblings,
disappeared into the wallpaper

a black mound of sugar,
hysterically unhappy
but polite

I imagine her on a snow bank,
on a soft sound—
all pearls and pressed dresses

the way angels laugh
themselves asleep.

Afraid, I stop,
then keep repeating murder,
a convulsive gesture,

my words lining your belly
like snakes,   like knives.

Lovely, forgotten,
regrettable.

Bite your tongue,
remember   the taste of arsenic,
the question of
hardly breathing.

You should be ashamed,
tempted, the memory of almost dying
an absolute merriment,
    a sobering loneliness

it happened in the house
your lips sugar, silent
the family gathering
in sobering prayer

    on this—the subject of blackberries

such lack of human discipline
through dark gates of death

I, a frightful madam,
might start thinking about

suffering. How it climbs
through mouths, a black cat,
an accused stranger.

I survive the newspapers,
the sensationalized flattery
of victims   exhaustive
in their living.

I devour the pocketbooks
of curious women, such passion

in scenes of rude questioning,
on witness stands made of
tragedy, blessed

with disagreement. I sit
acquitted at your table, my name
a doorway,

a disturbance.

Walk past me, timid:
my face
able to speak openly
about the delicate
jawline   of a woman

how a portrait of spells
lies underneath her skin:

petal-pressed yet   threatening
the bite before the blood.

She put on gloves,
hid wildness beneath
hemlock and small
summer delicacies.

I ate meals of thornapple,
licked paralysis
into squares of velvet grass,
her meal a punishment,
the root of rich mushrooms,
forced casting,

her intention a blind trial,
the weather hoarse
against the sound of
spiced baneberry
simmering   in the pot.

Destroy us all blindly
each smile a small shudder,
a gesture of blood   masquerading
as wild strawberries.

The teapot screams, rose-colored
against boiled spiders, the sympathy
of rats,   a chance display
of taxidermy, unanswered self-pity.

   I'd never killed anyone before.

Such a quiet body
twisted in great pain,   overstaying
its welcome, losing
track of time…

I pretended not to understand

III

Three times I came to tea,
bent toward trees like
a tired Saturday morning,
my mother   a storm,
one quick ripple:
    deep, restless.

At night, we spoke of omens,
they called to me, dressed
in locked doors, hanging
like loose wires: a safeguard
in a river run dry.

I checked beds,
buried dragons
in the attic, my teeth
a powerful ribbon,
a necklace worn
by hidden trees, a jewel
of torn pleasure,
I screamed six silver nails,
gave them each
your name.

I carried knives
bright and clean, washed
the cellar of pride, supplied
it with jars of mother's milk:
    the last, undrinkable,
    her life an uncompromising rot

preserved   like apple jelly.

I never touched anything
difficult to eat: that first heart,
the hot milk of lies—

my tray, a concerned note of
opened wounds, wandering darkness,
the dying body
of a forever poem.

Instead   feed me
with first light, spilled crumbs,
the wetness of woods,

    dark green and amber,
    I sense a change coming
     from the ground.

I carried dandelion greens
to the moon, drank the magic
of powerful words, the company
of fools singing, sleeping alongside
stalks of rhubarb, their arrival soft,
a gentle kneeling
on flesh, on glass.

I slept with the thought
of a head once, the off-key noise
of fractures an easy wife to bed:
the last day of pain
an earthly premonition—

such whistling,　　　　　whistling,
a never-ending *please come home*.

My last breakfast—

a meal of fried boy, the dripping
state of grudges, a closing
smile on rare chills

sat heavy somewhere, frowning,
folded under a chestnut tree, the lost hours
of his life a dropped twig,
a tasteless book, a few minutes
of chewing before bed.

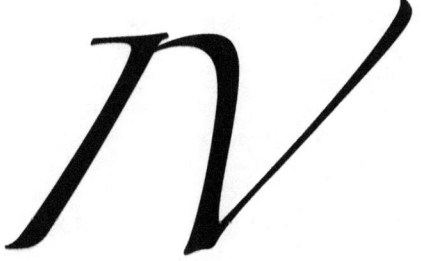

Into an air of change, I lay
like fog refusing the clouds
underneath my boots, my hand
held against the thin things
with splintered hair,
their watchful gaze
a sliced shadow   on creeping walls,
a crooked ocean waving
to a doll with your face.

Perhaps tomorrow,
in a slow black rain,
I'll shut out the souvenirs
of broken windows and
stolen flowers, release
the cries of murders
in each unguarded shiver
drowning   near the creek.

I'll listen to stories
of cats nailed to pine trees,
keep a record of names—
the ones that hide
like thick gloves
or suitcases full of hunger.

Then

I'll softly kill
a nest of secrets, remake
the orchard with snakes,
mouths open, bodies writhing,
the hiss comes straight
from your throat.

They never opened my calls
to death, the orphanage embarrassed,
my writing a faint rain of wishes,
unanswered letters. I parked my feet
outside their window,

    stood watching, wrote
their names in dust on the driveway.

I leaned against the killings, a picnic
of blank faces, their hands
barely touching, a tight wound
that spilled no answers. I couldn't breathe,
kept the shades drawn,

    a safe darkness, the kiss
    of crowded warmth.

Hunt me, I dare you.

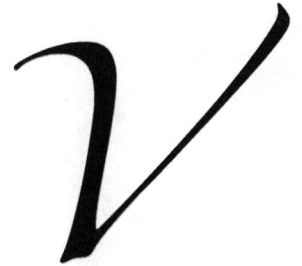

Awakened, a trailing mist
hugs my morning tea,
an early love, shining

        venomous

there is a red rose-petal breakfast
listening on the lawn, a feathered
spoon resting in a sunlit doorway

&

I am the ghost   responsible
for all that fell apart, a blank page,
the smashed table, scattered

        splintered

I drink the absence of color, taste
the late fee for my refusal to smile,
three times and it's real. No more
running:

his name already
on my lips.

A promise to leave,   the night
a swept pile of glass stuck
glittering in my teeth: feral,
this lingering sparkle, my laugh
an outright lie.

It was unpleasant, your beauty
an arranged anticipation   that
counted down with each look
    your grace a confession,
      an impossible conversation

I dreamt of filling you
with the voice of pity,
with all things terribly bad.

To anticipate the details
of a curious trial, I melt
into suspicion, the severed wealth
of dead family a romantic room
dressed for company
on my face.

We don't see life in this room,
his name still unsafe to speak.

I blink, turn away,
the memory of birthdays
spilling on the floor.

I laugh but I'm afraid,
the cross of swallowed pieces
a delicious garden spreading
in my chest.

In the event of a delicate stomach
I cut the pieces small, an eagerness
to keep him talking, to imagine
the hesitation of fingers
down my throat.

I gesture in anger, my voice
a shaking of sorry brought on
by the sight of his liver:

>   my lunch swelling,
>   begging "no" beneath
>   the knife.

I wash myself with pearls,
the ugliness of erased magic
a severed salamander, the slip
beneath a too-thin dress.

Mother's diamond ring sits
on a pair of witches, their brooms
a flying harp, a wedding song,
the pride of polished teacups
hovering over mud.

Later on, I lick the backs
of wooden chairs, the smoke
in the attic the perfect guest
for wide-eyed spirits, their acts
disagreeable to men.

>   I watch the birds attempt
>   magic. Decide to eat them
>   nevertheless.

Three days of biting, of blotting
the faces of soft things, I eat
the wet parts inside, recall
a time when I disliked
people watching.

    I laugh in red, the first
    symptom of violence.

Oh,   *I'm quite comfortable now.*

VI

The house was not a key
to pay for hate. Perhaps
it belonged   to the dance of ghosts,
all those secrets lodged
in dresser drawers,
in congested
basements I dared not
visit.

Perhaps it possessed
the cipher for the speech
of crows, the door
a message   three knocks,
a sunrise hidden in
the signature of
beasts.

Still,

I crawl on hands
made of gingerbread,
ask the old witch
for a library of truths,

no more false gods,
villages of fire.

I want the skeletons
of Tuesday mornings
wise, free.

    I'll shatter them all.

I noticed a hand   inside the chair
a watch ticking, ticking
to the sound of guilt. Leather, gold,
I pressed it against my throat,
a stamp. Curled its five-finger imprint
around words bred from fear.

A patient woman, I created
these maps to hell, slept in
chains made of cold fathers,
wandered woods, the bodies
of frozen birds bulging
beneath my shirt.

Do you think they'll come
for me? I write my tragedies,
swallow tongues just in case:
     flaccid, thick.

They sit in me like tepid
jewels. Such value in the stolen,
in all things ripped away.

Everywhere in the house
I smelled the echo   of leaving,
the sound of burnt matches
cheerful like a rejection,
the way sickness hides
in the lungs.

I try to correct the past,
run wild with the wish
of lost anger, the hospital
a distant memory, a broken
arm stuffed between the
sheets.

A strange landscape, the look
in his eyes: two black buttons,
a dark pool. Bewitched, I laugh
in feathers,

    the pillow, so soft
    against his face.

I didn't mean to feed on him: the wet slap
of blood, the crunch and grind of teeth.
    Coffee like tar, like oil
mixed sunny-side up
with sweet meats   cooked
in honey-roasted
shame.

I sit in the kitchen, a slave
to the quiet dark, the hole
gnawing   at my chest:
the sleeping tangle of hunger
growing, a demon always
in the same
voice.

The dishonesty of disguise picks
at me, my true form a cackle
peeling from the walls. I submit
to apologies written in rows of
untouched trees, sink into laughter
flowing gently into clouds,

awake, dreaming. I listen to
prayers strung together by
bluebells and birch, promise
the spirits the taste of
wedding cake, the irony
of my grandfather's pipe.

Look for me in the wilted,
my body a dance of delicate
lace, the spider's web, the way
all things die breathless
and afraid.

VII

I suspect the cracks are opening,
the morning, a stiff drink   hammering
pounding away at the scream
in my chest.

    Just light the match, pray—

There's no way to touch this
attic in my head.

Perhaps I'll sleep on a bed of shattered glass,
read the books of empty minds,
shut myself away in a room without noise,

                              [without people]

just torn curtains,
half-peeled wallpaper—

    this existence, the song of
    all buried things.

Ever the fly to the spider's web,
I toss and turn on wet grass, my body
a banquet of dirt, a feast of witch tongues
and wolf livers, these scratches
a handwritten note to disturbed earth,
to the moment I stoned myself,
cursed this village the site of plague.

To speak thinly, honestly
on the matter of ghosts, my voice
a trapped laugh, the quiet chirp of
crickets—
I watch them linger
in the corner of your yard:
    a snowflake, a lily,
these bringers of poison, such
small whispering deaths.

Desire festers in the dark wounds
of mad sisters, the rot of their bones
a feast worthy of nature's crooked
teeth.

They quarrel with the scattered
cries of dying deer: threatening,
answering, the low growl of
Hell a warm meal,

> the spice left
> in the tea.

Pay attention to evil, the kitchen
a language of fabricated apologies
its hunger like a ravenous bear
clawing at the center of my chest:

    I am selfish with my death,
my name a severance to demons
locked up in trunks, their promises
sweet, sugar-spun lies.

They'll try to tell you I'm gone,
my inheritance a family plot, the
wrappings of my late mother's
dress:

    But I linger. Every window
a reflection of forgotten crimes,
misplaced rage, the leaves in the teacup
wet, the earth still weeping, reaching
for my hand.

To survive the furious arrangement
of misplaced bones, she believed
in the twist and turns of spines,
the snap of necks: bodies limp,
lifeless, like overgrown graves.

She rubbed her hands in dirt,
two maggots wedged between
her teeth, a waterfall of rats
in the basement: the dampness
of infestation hot on her lips.

It wouldn't be long before the
rot of coffins planted teeth in
the garden, poisoned the well
with the names of murdered
family, their voices soft, a lullaby
of lambs and ferns, the whispers
saying

> *eat them, savor them*
> *devour them all*

VIII

I washed out the space in my head
guarding my temper. The tricks stored
in dresser drawers crept burning
through the bedroom, my familiar
a chipped pipe wet beneath the
sheets.

I wrapped curtains around my chest,
a host of fragile cracks scattered
along every angle, my body
disarranged, a dowry left crawling
with the filth of time.

Sometimes I removed my eyes
only to throw myself down
the stairs, turned the stove on
just to smell the smoke. Tell me:
do you know what it's like to
swallow fire only to never
feel yourself burn?

Hysteria runs in the black
of my bile, a botched shriek
crashing into walls. With a fist,
it presses pale noise into my ears,
the filth of uncomfortable women
visible beneath the crowd's
disgusted laughs.

She identified with the face
in the creek, how it braided
an anonymous guilt
through rooms wrapped
in flames: the distant singing
of smothered children a vision
stamped on clouded windows,
the sharpness of rocks sticking
out of small bodies made of ash
a picture of devilry.

The quiet kill of stars pushes darkness
on the grass, a cautious following
of moss-drenched shadows telling stories
of blankets and waiting, how we die
a thousand deaths watching the leaves
change, the berries brighten—

> time, both everlasting
> and already gone.

With shattered hands, the laughter
of horrible stars cried into tea cups,
ran its night noise over broken chairs,
the sound of slaps a tattoo on her face.

    She ran to the woods, to the safety
    of crazed devils, her heart a brick,
    a boneyard of funeral shawls, the music
    of lost daughters shoved somewhere
    deep in her throat.

The forest danced to the greed of sleep,
the circle of trees a forgotten home, the ground
a killing silence, polite but begging,
desperate to be touched.

IX

The night took memories away—
erased faces, turned voices distant,
hid them all in the agonized burls
of arthritic trees.

We were but a closed door,
a subdued fawn, the woods hungry,
starving for bodies of small,
wicked girls.

Standing there, an abandoned girl
left to her tower, I return to the fire,
a visage of moving smoke:
black, ash—
    the word *water*
    dry on my lips.

I think about having tea in the creek,
starving myself in the trees. Tell me:

> Would you look for me in the garden?
> Search for me beneath the floors?

These dreams of dirt form burials
in my gut, twist golems into
my arms, the sad screech of birth
a familiar nightmare. I wonder:

> Would you hunt me in the woods?
> Chase me through the attic?

It's getting darker in my head,
this shame, an ugliness living in
windows, dancing inside the face
of broken mirrors. Promise me:

> You'll break down the walls.
> Rip out the floor.

Find me.
Don't let me stay here

Don't let me be alone.

I taste how you shivered,
how you dissolved
into the attic: half solid,
your left side ripped out,
the scent of scattered death
on the floor.

You begged like an abused
dog, intestines leaking,
a mess of cracked eggs,
spilled sugar, your body
an imprint of what it means
to try but fail.

Forget about the teeth
in your neck, the misunderstood
harm of lilies pinned to your hands—
it's the gash in your stomach
you need to worry about, the death line
on your palm. Trust me when I say
I've buried countless bodies
in my mouth, their screams

        blackberry cobbler,
        a cold, sugared tea.

I wake to a procession of knives,
the dance of uneasy dreams
an untouched murder postponed
by the wet silver of coins.

    It hangs, a noose,
    the witch swinging
    in the trees.

A broken saucer holds a teacup
of urine, the hooks in my feet
rusted, heavy. I itch the roots
of screaming rage, an untuned
harp crying against silent skies.

    We collapse, a castle
    of dead women
    crawling on the floor.

There are worse things than
burning alive, our generation
trauma-soaked, blind
eager to thank
the match.

It was noon when I ate
the raw hearts of chickens,
hunted grasshoppers with the
wrong end of my broom. I rubbed
eggs over my body, licked the salt
behind my grandmother's ear,
walked backwards out the kitchen
counting, checking, the death rattles
of my family ringing in my ears.

There were two cups of sleep
hidden under the stairs, my mattress
stuffed with newspaper headlines,
yellow flowers, the rabbit foot
I chewed off when the sun
went away.

Do you think I'm safe with these
dirty hands? The nails in my palms
a locked door, an extinguished flame,
the almost-ashes a protective garden,
a barricade against a sister's sin.

But I know I'm guilty, a promise
made between toxins and last words,
coughing, choking, your safeguards
mean nothing, my face a funeral
of mistaken obligations. I'll sleep
soundly driving you away.

You soak beneath the floorboards, a sick
footstep, a doll silently coming back
to life. I breathe in the absence of you:
wicked, wanting, the soft moss
of your pale flesh a comfort
that weeps into the ground.

x

Thin shapes, narrow, disguised
awakened near the exposed cracks,
the faceless children back, active
the broken necks of birds
like stillborns   on the porch.

The barricades scrambled, my mouth
a dark bath of emeralds, the forest
laughing, climbing behind the
dead spots in my eyes.

I ate the house, devoured the smoke
licked berries from the vents,

                      [but I hesitated]

the strangled sheets of yesterday's
wash a noose, a necklace. Mother
told me to run, hid me in cellars
told me to remember the quiet,
the drip

        drop

            slap

of hateful watching. I slept

in baskets woven from human
hair, threatened by the softness
of feathers. When winter came,
I sewed the hole in my head,
begged for the belt against
my back.

Wearing the skin of candlelight, I suffer
the summer moons, vanish in the softness
of empty knocks, the sad laughter of dolls
riding the walls like ghosts—

>these spirits, such intruders
>they listen like mad wolves.

Roasted flesh, the warmth of cinnamon,
I poked cloves through their eyelids,
covered their lips in foil. My church
became the sound of baking, my shame
celebrated somewhere between
the molasses, the cut of harp strings.

I made certain the vines tore into
their mouths, evil those marks of
lovely rage. A tomb, carved. A spell,
cast. Inside me, I ripped snakes from
a well of defiance. A gluttonous pig,
I ate their faces.

Do you tend to the funeral of moons?
Visit the lost sisters, the demons
dancing in the woods? They say
there are doors to our graves,
small openings smiling
on the wrong side of death, the echoes
of empty laughter a spirit haunting
the hallways of ruined women,
barefoot maids: their magic, a black widow,
a familiar terror known only to men.

About the Author

Stephanie M. Wytovich is an American poet, novelist, and essayist. Her work has been showcased in numerous magazines and anthologies such as *Weird Tales, Nightmare Magazine, Southwest Review, Year's Best Hardcore Horror: Volume 2, The Best Horror of the Year: Volume 8 & 15*, as well as many others.

Wytovich is the Poetry Editor for Raw Dog Screaming Press, and an adjunct at Western Connecticut State University, Southern New Hampshire University, and Point Park University. She is a recipient of the Elizabeth Matchett Stover Memorial Award, the 2021 Ladies of Horror Fiction Writers Grant, and has received the Rocky Wood Memorial Scholarship for non-fiction writing.

Wytovich is a member of the Science Fiction Poetry Association, an active member of the Horror Writers Association, and a graduate of Seton Hill University's MFA program for Writing Popular Fiction. Her Bram Stoker Award-winning poetry collection, *Brothel*, earned a home with Raw Dog Screaming Press alongside *Hysteria: A Collection of Madness, Mourning Jewelry, An Exorcism of Angels, Sheet*

Music to My Acoustic Nightmare, The Apocalyptic Mannequin, and most recently, *On the Subject of Blackberries.* Her debut novel, *The Eighth,* is published with Dark Regions Press, and her nonfiction craft book for speculative poetry, *Writing Poetry in the Dark,* wherever books are sold.

Follow Wytovich at http://stephaniewytovich.blogspot.com/ and on Twitter and Instagram @SWytovich and @thehauntedbookshelf. You can also find her essays, nonfiction, and class offerings on LitReactor.

www.ingramcontent.com/pod-product-compliance
Lightning Source LLC
LaVergne TN
LVHW041339080426
835512LV00006B/536